Plant Hope

Also by Alexandra Vasiliu

Blooming: *Poems on Love, Self-Discovery, and Femininity*

Healing Words: *A Poetry Collection for Broken Hearts*

Be My Moon: *A Poetry Collection for Romantic Souls*

Plant Hope
A Journal for Healing

Alexandra Vasiliu

Stairway Books
Boston

Plant Hope: A Journal for Healing by Alexandra Vasiliu. Boston: Stairway Books, 2021

Editing services provided by Melanie Underwood at www.melanieunderwood.co.uk
Cover Illustration and Image Quotes: Natalie Osipova via www.shutterstock.com

ISBN-13: 9798597418667

*To those who need
to heal and grow*

WELCOME TO
YOUR HEALING JOURNEY

First, let me start with a small confession: there is no magic pill for heartbreak. This is the naked truth. You stand in the arena of your life. Lions surround you. They look straight in your eyes. You know them. They are your fears, your anxieties, your pains. You cannot avoid them. You cannot make them disappear. You cannot make your heart feel less pain or no pain at all.

There is only one thing you can do. Fight. This is the secret power of healing.

Enter the arena of your life and look straight in the eyes of those lions. Although they are untamed, don't run. Be brave and fight. Knock them down.

There is no magic pill that will make this fight easier or shorter. No pill. Empower yourself and take the dare: fight back.

This healing journal comes as your helper. It is your armor to guard you in your battle. It is your tool that will guide you to gather wisdom, strength, hope, courage, inspiration, and self-confidence. It is your secret power to help you rise from the ashes and win. Use it.

Journal your thoughts as desperately, as fiercely, as sincerely as you feel. Draw pictures expressing your feelings. Answer these questions in the order that fits your needs. Each page is dedicated to you. Each question is waiting for you. Be honest with yourself. Stay connected with your heart. Try to dig deeper and deeper, permit your words to express your deepest feelings so that you can heal your hidden wounds, find your strengths, win back your dreams, and claim your authenticity.

Plant hope in your heart's wounds, wait for love to grow, and allow yourself to rise again like a beautiful phoenix.

Love,
Alexandra

Plant Hope

You become what you believe

WHO ARE YOU?

I am a love poem
in the human body.

Take your time and write down everything about
who you are, who you were, and who you dream of
becoming. Be honest.

**When you think of yourself, the first thing that
comes to your mind is:**

Strong & enduring

What is unique about yourself?

Care so much about others
determined
Biased (usually)
motivated

What story do you tell yourself about yourself?

That I struggle, don't feel good
enough. Others take advantage,
take me for granted.
Care too much.

Check your favorite affirmation.
I am defined by:
- o **my profession**
- o **my faith**
- o **my family**
- o **my friends**
- o **my aspirations**
- o **my failures**

Now please journal your thoughts.

None of those.
Defined by my fitness.

What more do you want people to know about you? Why?

_____

_____

_____

_____

Check the affirmations that touch your heart.
- ☞ **I am the sum of all the things that happened to me.**
- ○ **I am the sum of all the things that I have dreamed of.**
- ○ **I am the sum of all the things that I chose.**
- ○ **I am the sum of all the people that I loved.**

Journal your thoughts.

_____

_____

_____

_____

_____

_____

_____

_____

_____

_____

List your ten main qualities.

- ○ **1.**
- ○ **2.**
- ○ **3.**
- ○ **4.**
- ○ **5.**
- ○ **6.**
- ○ **7.**
- ○ **8.**
- ○ **9.**
- ○ **10.**

What is the quality that you aim to embody one day? Journal your thoughts.

_____

_____

_____

_____

_____

_____

_____

_____

_____

What are your greatest shortcomings?

What are your weaknesses?

What are your strengths?

What is your biggest disappointment?

_____

_____

_____

_____

_____

What is your most significant achievement?

_____

_____

_____

_____

_____

Name eight things that you think you are worthy of having.

- o **1.**
- o **2.**
- o **3.**
- o **4.**
- o **5.**
- o **6.**
- o **7.**
- o **8.**

Check your favorite affirmation.
- o **I am a love poem in the human body.**
- o **I am a ray of hope.**
- o **I am a flower of grace.**
- o **I am a dream seeded in this world.**
- o **I am a song waiting for its musician.**

Now please add your affirmations.

I am...

_____

_____

_____

I am...

_____

_____

_____

Journal your thoughts about who you want to become one day.

_____

_____

_____

_____

_____

_____

_____

YOUR HEART

Feel welcome in your heart.
You are not a stranger.

Your heart is the most precious treasure that you have. Let's talk now about your inner gem!

Check the affirmation that most resonates with you. Then, journal your thoughts.
- ○ **I feel connected with my heart.**
- ○ **I have lost touch with my heart.**

_____

_____

_____

_____

_____

If you feel connected with your heart, describe the best way that helps you communicate with your inner self.

_____

_____

_____

_____

_____

If you feel that you have lost touch with your heart, describe the best way that could help you rekindle this relationship.

_____

_____

_____

_____

_____

Do you believe that your heart is beautiful? Why? Journal your thoughts.

_____

_____

_____

_____

_____

Do you feel that your heart is still young? Why? Journal your thoughts.

_____

_____

_____

_____

_____

What is the superpower of your heart?

_____

_____

_____

_____

_____

_____

What do you see when you look at yourself in the mirror? Journal your thoughts.

_____

_____

_____

_____

_____

_____

_____

_____

_____

_____

_____

How does your heart look like right now? Use just one word. Jot it down.

_____

_____

Imagine a magical mirror in which you could see your heart. What would you like to see in this unique mirror? Journal your thoughts.

_____

_____

_____

_____

_____

_____

_____

_____

_____

_____

_____

_____

_____

_____

**Do you think that you are emotionally mature?
Journal your thoughts.**

_____

_____

_____

_____

_____

_____

_____

**Dream of something beneficial to your heart.
Journal your thoughts.**

_____

_____

_____

_____

_____

_____

_____

_____

_____

What is the kindest thing that you would say to your heart? Journal your thoughts.

_____

_____

_____

_____

_____

_____

_____

_____

_____

Water the garden of your heart with five positive words. Then, journal your thoughts.

- o **1.**
- o **2.**
- o **3.**
- o **4.**
- o **5.**

_____

_____

_____

_____

_____

Check the most relevant affirmation.

- ○ **I want my heart to be a poem.**
- ○ **I want my heart to be a song.**
- ○ **I want my heart to be a piece of art.**
- ○ **I want my heart to be a flower.**
- ○ **I want my heart to be an eagle.**

Now journal your thoughts.

_____

_____

_____

_____

_____

Write two ways in which you can show love to your heart. Journal your thoughts.

_____

_____

_____

_____

_____

_____

_____

_____

_____

What do you do to protect your heart?

_____

_____

_____

_____

_____

_____

_____

How much time do you spend talking with your heart? Journal your thoughts.

_____

_____

_____

_____

_____

_____

_____

_____

_____

There is no other place
where you should be right now
than your heart.
If you want to heal your wounds,
be present in your heart.

What is the question that you have never wanted to ask yourself?

_____

_____

_____

_____

_____

_____

_____

_____

What is your heart saying to you right now?

_____

_____

_____

_____

_____

_____

_____

_____

_____

_____

What is the question that you have always wanted to ask your heart? Why?

_____

_____

_____

_____

_____

_____

_____

What is the thought that pulls you out of bed every morning? Journal your thoughts.

_____

_____

_____

_____

_____

_____

_____

_____

Complete the following sentences as you wish.
- Every day I make room in my heart for...

- In my heart there is no...

- In my heart, I carry only...

- Every day my heart is full of...

- My heart doesn't...

Write down the quote that had the most impact on you. Journal your thoughts.

_____

_____

_____

_____

_____

_____

_____

_____

Do you hide a short poem deep down in your heart? Write it below.

_____

_____

_____

_____

_____

_____

_____

_____

_____

_____

Create a short poem that can represent you.

_____

_____

_____

_____

_____

_____

_____

_____

_____

Write down the best way of helping your heart spread light and love.

_____

_____

_____

_____

_____

_____

_____

_____

_____

_____

List ten words that make your heart feel better.

    ○ **1.**   ○ **6.**

    ○ **2.**   ○ **7.**

    ○ **3.**   ○ **8.**

    ○ **4.**   ○ **9.**

    ○ **5.**   ○ **10**

Journal your thoughts.

_____

_____

_____

_____

List ten words that have always hurt your heart.

    ○ **1.**   ○ **6.**

    ○ **2.**   ○ **7.**

    ○ **3.**   ○ **8.**

    ○ **4.**   ○ **9.**

    ○ **5.**   ○ **10**

Journal your thoughts.

_____

_____

_____

_____

What wounds do you carry in your heart?

_____

_____

_____

_____

_____

_____

_____

_____

_____

What is hurting your heart right now? Why? Journal your thoughts.

_____

_____

_____

_____

_____

_____

_____

_____

_____

How can you make your heart bloom again?

_____

_____

_____

_____

_____

_____

What is the language that your heart speaks every day?
- o My heart speaks the language of love.
- o My heart speaks the language of kindness.
- o My heart speaks the language of forgiveness.
- o My heart speaks the language of anger.

Now journal your thoughts.

_____

_____

_____

_____

_____

_____

_____

_____

_____

_____

Check your favorite affirmation.
- o **I want my heart to become fluent in kindness.**
- o **I want my heart to become fluent in empathy.**
- o **I want my heart to become fluent in love.**

Now journal your thoughts.

And in the end
let kindness be
the language of your heart.

If you could seed flowers in your heart, what type of flowers would you choose? Why? Draw them below.

Imagine a flower of hope growing beautifully within your heart. Please express your feelings in a drawing below.

If you could give a beautiful name to your heart, which one would you choose? Use one word. Then, journal your thoughts.

_____

_____

_____

_____

Check your favorite affirmation.
- ○ **From now on, I want to feed my heart with hope.**
- ○ **From now on, I want to feed my heart with love.**
- ○ **From now on, I want to feed my heart with wisdom.**
- ○ **From now on, I want to feed my heart with joy.**

Now journal your thoughts.

_____

_____

_____

_____

_____

_____

_____

_____

*Let joy be
your heart's name.*

What emotional health advice would you give to your heart? Journal your thoughts.

_____

_____

_____

_____

_____

_____

_____

_____

**Complete the following sentences as you wish.
Dear Heart, from now on...**

_____

_____

_____

_____

Dear Heart, let's...

_____

_____

_____

_____

_____

Dear Heart, in the coming year...

_____

_____

_____

_____

_____

Dear Heart, I will...

_____

_____

_____

_____

Dear Heart, I will strive to...

_____

_____

_____

_____

Dear Heart, I promise...

_____

_____

_____

_____

_____

YOUR PAST PATTERNS
Your past is a dead city.

We always visit the past like we would go to our homeland. Don't hide yourself. Don't be afraid. Let's talk about your past.

Choose your favorite affirmation.
Thinking of my past makes my heart feel:
- o **light**
- o **heavy**
- o **embarrassed**
- o **proud**
- o **happy**
- o **sad**
- o **warm**
- o **nostalgic**
- o **angry**

Now journal your thoughts.

_____

_____

_____

_____

_____

_____

_____

_____

How do you think that your past experiences shaped your heart? Journal your thoughts.

**Rewrite the story of your past experiences.
Change the ending to a positive perspective.**

What is your biggest regret?

How do you think you would be without
carrying this regret? Journal your thoughts.

Make a list of five things from your past that still hurt you.

- 1.

- 2.

- 3.

- 4.

- 5.

What painful memories do you want to dispel from your heart? Why? Journal your thoughts.

_____

_____

_____

_____

_____

_____

_____

_____

_____

_____

_____

_____

_____

What is your greatest mistake so far?

_____

_____

_____

_____

_____

_____

Can you forgive yourself for making mistakes? Journal your thoughts.

_____

_____

_____

_____

_____

Can you accept your past mistakes? Why? Journal your thoughts.

_____

_____

_____

_____

_____

Can you make peace with your past and move on? Why? Journal your thoughts.

_____

_____

_____

_____

List three things from your past that still cause you low self-esteem. Journal your thoughts.

- 1.

- 2.

- 3.

_____

_____

_____

_____

_____

_____

_____

_____

_____

List three things from your past that you need to overcome. Journal your thoughts.

- 1.
- 2.
- 3.

_____

_____

_____

_____

_____

If you could change one thing from your past, what would it be?

_____

_____

_____

_____

_____

_____

_____

_____

If you could get back one thing from your past, what would it be? Journal your thoughts.

_____

_____

_____

_____

_____

_____

_____

If you could go back in time, what would you tell your younger self?

_____

_____

_____

_____

_____

_____

_____

_____

Make a list of your past experiences that you would like to live again. Journal your thoughts.

_____

_____

_____

_____

_____

_____

_____

_____

Make a list of the things from your past that you would do differently. Journal your thoughts.

_____

_____

_____

_____

_____

_____

_____

_____

_____

How do you refrain from falling back into the patterns of your past?

_____

_____

_____

_____

_____

_____

_____

What is the recurring pattern of your past that you would like to change?

_____

_____

_____

_____

_____

_____

_____

_____

_____

Describe the best strategy that brings yourself back to the present moment.

_____

_____

_____

_____

_____

_____

_____

_____

Create a short poem that can help you embrace your past and face it with peace and resilience.

_____

_____

_____

_____

_____

_____

_____

_____

_____

_____

What have you learned from your past so far? Be true without holding back.

Imagine that you could plant the special flower of self-acceptance in the soil of your past. Draw this flower below.

Draw a mesmerizing flower that can heal your emotional pains.

TOXIC THOUGHTS

*If you want to heal
your heart's wounds,
start healing your thoughts.*

Toxic thoughts are like a slow poison. Let's stop
them now.

**Do you think that your toxic thoughts dictate the
story of your life? Journal your thoughts.**

_____

_____

_____

_____

_____

**How do you feel when you are sunk in toxic
thoughts? Journal your thoughts.**

_____

_____

_____

_____

_____

What are the toxic thoughts that you are struggling with right now? List them below.

Do you believe that overthinking and perfectionism fuel your toxic thoughts?

When you struggle with toxic thoughts, how do you navigate towards inner peace?

_____

_____

_____

_____

_____

_____

_____

Describe your best strategy to stop the toxic friction in your mind.

_____

_____

_____

_____

_____

_____

_____

_____

_____

Imagine that toxic thoughts are like weeds. Draw your weedy, untidy, unhealthy thoughts below.

Stop the downward spiral of your toxic thoughts through these empowering affirmations. Please check your favorite one.

- o I am rising above my misfortunes.
- o I am healing.
- o I am changing.
- o I am fighting.
- o I am growing.
- o I am strong.
- o I will not give up hope.

Now journal your thoughts.

Read the example below and complete the following sentences with positive affirmations.
When you think, 'I am down,' say to yourself, 'One day, I will rise again.'

When you think, 'I am afraid,' say to yourself…

_____

_____

_____

_____

_____

When you think, 'I am not worthy of love,' say to yourself…

_____

_____

_____

_____

_____

When you think, 'Nobody loves me,' say to yourself…

_____

_____

_____

_____

_____

MY TRAUMA
Heal your pain.

Dealing with trauma means you don't feel free any longer. Let's talk and change this from now on!

What is the story of your trauma?

_____

_____

_____

_____

_____

_____

_____

_____

_____

_____

_____

_____

_____

_____

_____

_____

_____

Do you think that you indulged yourself in suffering too much? Journal your thoughts.

_____

_____

_____

_____

_____

_____

_____

_____

_____

_____

_____

_____

Could you frame your trauma in five words? Please write them down.

- 1.
- 2.
- 3.
- 4.
- 5.

What is hurting you right now?

_____

_____

_____

_____

_____

_____

_____

_____

How do you feel about the person who hurt you the most? Please be honest.

_____

_____

_____

_____

_____

_____

What is the name of the person whose painful fingerprints are all over your heart?

_____

_____

Can you forgive the person who hurt you? Why?

_____

_____

_____

_____

Do you think you need to forgive or to forget that person? Journal your thoughts.

_____

_____

_____

_____

_____

_____

_____

_____

What would you tell that person if you were face-to-face?

_____

_____

_____

Imagine how you would be without your trauma. Journal your thoughts.

_____

_____

_____

_____

_____

_____

_____

_____

Do you think that your trauma is a toxic thing in your life? Journal your thoughts.

_____

_____

_____

_____

_____

_____

_____

_____

_____

Do you think that trauma is an open door for self-growth? Journal your thoughts.

_____

_____

_____

_____

_____

_____

_____

_____

_____

Do you think that your trauma puts you into survival mode? Journal your thoughts.

_____

_____

_____

_____

_____

_____

_____

_____

_____

Do you think that your trauma makes your life stagnant? Journal your thoughts.

_____

_____

_____

_____

_____

_____

_____

Your trauma is not a hindrance to becoming a stronger person. Journal your thoughts.

_____

_____

_____

_____

_____

_____

_____

_____

_____

Write down, 'I am more than my trauma.' Then, journal your thoughts.

I am more than...

_____

_____

_____

I am more than...

_____

_____

_____

I am more than...

_____

_____

_____

I am more than...

_____

_____

_____

If your trauma brings to life fears, blow them away with one word. Write this word in uppercase letters.

_____

_____

Are you ready to fight with your insecurities and your past ghosts? Journal your thoughts.

_____

_____

_____

_____

_____

_____

_____

What is your strategy for better coping with anxiety when you face the ghosts of your past?

_____

_____

_____

_____

_____

_____

_____

_____

_____

If the ghosts of your past were living people, what would you tell them?

_____

_____

_____

_____

_____

What would you say to yourself to alleviate your fears? Please use empowering words.

_____

_____

_____

_____

_____

What can comfort you when you feel helpless?

_____

_____

_____

_____

_____

List the first three fears that you want to overcome. Then, journal your thoughts.

- ○ 1.
- ○ 2.
- ○ 3.

_____

_____

_____

_____

_____

Complete the following sentences.
When I overcome one of my fears, I will feel...

_____

_____

_____

In the coming months, I want to overcome...

_____

_____

_____

When I overcome my trauma, I will feel...

_____

_____

_____

Do you feel emotionally mature enough to overcome your trauma and move on with your life? Journal your thoughts.

_____

_____

_____

_____

_____

_____

What are you searching for right now?

_____

_____

_____

_____

_____

What stops you from finding inner peace?

_____

_____

_____

_____

_____

What would make you feel secure? Why?

_____

_____

_____

_____

_____

_____

What do you need most when you struggle with your trauma?

_____

_____

_____

_____

_____

List five new daily habits that can help you overcome trauma.

- ○ 1.
- ○ 2.
- ○ 3.
- ○ 4.
- ○ 5.

Write down two strategies that rejuvenate your heart when you feel emotionally exhausted.

_____

_____

_____

_____

_____

_____

_____

_____

_____

_____

If you could seed a value in someone's heart who struggles with trauma, what would you choose?

_____

_____

_____

_____

_____

_____

_____

_____

_____

If you could plant a flower in someone's heart who struggles with trauma, what sort of flower would you choose? Why? Please draw it below.

believe in YOURSELF

LETTING GO

I want to learn the art
of letting go and being free.

Letting go is an important life lesson. Let's dive into its meanings!

For me, 'letting go' means...

_____

_____

_____

_____

_____

What stops you from letting go?
- ○ **My ego**
- ○ **My anxiety**
- ○ **My pride**

Now please journal your thoughts.

_____

_____

_____

_____

_____

_____

_____

Check the affirmations that speak to you.
Letting go starts with:
- o self-respect
- o desire for freedom
- o willingness for healing
- o need for a change

Now journal your thoughts.

Check your favorite affirmation.
- ○ **Letting go is an art that I need to learn.**
- ○ **Letting go is a healthy habit that I should practice more.**
- ○ **Letting go is a therapeutical attitude that I should acquire.**

Journal your thoughts.

_____

_____

_____

_____

_____

_____

_____

_____

_____

_____

_____

_____

_____

_____

_____

_____

_____

_____

Complete the following sentences.
In the next months, I want to let go of...

_____

_____

_____

_____

_____

_____

_____

_____

When I let go of my past, I want to free myself
from...

_____

_____

_____

_____

_____

_____

_____

_____

_____

_____

Letting go implies:

- o **I stop controlling someone else.**
- o **I focus on my flaws.**
- o **I stop blaming myself.**
- o **I build self-respect**
- o **I learn to love myself first.**
- o **I cut off my dependency on other people.**
- o **I learn to be generous in an emotionally healthy way.**
- o **I pray more.**
- o **I learn to heal my heart.**
- o **I believe in my potential.**

Now journal your thoughts.

_____

_____

_____

_____

_____

_____

_____

_____

_____

_____

_____

_____

_____

HEALING MY WOUNDS
Healing my heart's wounds
is the best gift
that I can give to myself.

No matter how complicated your healing process is, never give up. Remind yourself, 'The greatest gift I can give to myself is healing my heart's wounds.'

What is the turning point in your life that made you decide to heal your heart's wounds?

Please give a name to your healing journey. Be as creative as you want.

_____

_____

_____

How do you feel about starting your healing process? Be honest.
- o I feel insecure.
- o I am a stranger to myself.
- o I am afraid.
- o I feel alone.
- o I feel hopeless.

Now journal your feelings below.

_____

_____

_____

_____

_____

_____

_____

_____

_____

_____

_____

_____

Healing,
growing,
and blooming
are my daily duties.

What are your plans for how to begin your healing journey?

_____

_____

_____

_____

_____

_____

_____

Check the most relevant affirmation to you.
- ○ **My fears dominate me.**
- ○ **My anxiety controls me.**
- ○ **My loneliness suffocates me.**
- ○ **My trauma weakens me.**

Now journal your thoughts.

_____

_____

_____

_____

_____

_____

_____

Check your favorite affirmation.

- ○ Healing begins with letting go of my past.
- ○ Healing means that I get to know myself better.
- ○ Healing is giving birth to the best version of myself.
- ○ Healing implies personal transformation and self-growth.
- ○ Healing is the most important gift I can give to myself.

Now journal your thoughts.

How do you manage your ups and downs during your healing process? Journal your thoughts.

Check your favorite affirmation.
Healing my heart's wounds is a sign of:
- ○ **self-love**
- ○ **courage**
- ○ **inner strength**
- ○ **wisdom**
- ○ **clarity**

Now journal your thoughts.

**Journal your thoughts about this affirmation,
'Healing comes with a personal transformation.'**

_____

_____

_____

_____

_____

_____

_____

_____

_____

**Do you feel you are ready for a personal
transformation? Journal your thoughts.**

_____

_____

_____

_____

_____

_____

_____

_____

_____

_____

What are you willing to change about yourself? Journal your thoughts.

_____

_____

_____

_____

_____

_____

_____

What is your narrative about healing your heart's wounds? Journal your thoughts.

_____

_____

_____

_____

_____

_____

_____

_____

_____

Check the affirmations that speak to your heart.
Healing my wounded heart means:
- o I will get as close as I can to my inner self.
- o I will embrace change.
- o I will never again hide from my pains.
- o I will nourish myself with love.
- o I will fight for myself.
- o I will make my life easier.

Now journal your thoughts.

_____

_____

_____

_____

_____

_____

_____

Journal your thoughts about this affirmation,
'Turn your pain into strength and hope.'

_____

_____

_____

_____

_____

_____

_____

Do you think that healing your trauma will make you a stronger person? Why?

Journal your thoughts about this affirmation, 'Pain is not my homeland.'

Check the goals that you want to achieve during your healing process.

- o **I will not seek validation anymore.**
- o **I will not seek approval anymore.**
- o **I will stop making others feel good to my detriment.**
- o **I will try to be useful to others, respecting myself first.**
- o **I will know myself better.**
- o **I will be more self-confident.**
- o **I will respect my worth.**
- o **I will protect my inner peace.**
- o **I will value my purity.**
- o **I will love my inner beauty.**
- o **I will remove all the superficial layers of my life.**
- o **I will find my vocation.**
- o **I will work hard on my dreams.**
- o **I will worship God.**
- o **I will pray more.**
- o **I will help others more.**
- o **I will be kind to others, knowing that I suffered a lot.**
- o **I will build and keep strong, positive, healthy relationships.**

Now write down your goals.

_____

_____

_____

_____

_____

Complete the following sentences.
After healing my heart's wounds, all I want:

- to do is...

_____

_____

_____

- to love is...

_____

_____

_____

- to learn is...

_____

_____

_____

- to have is...

_____

_____

_____

- to improve is...

_____

_____

_____

List five positive words that resonate with you.

- o 1.
- o 2.
- o 3.
- o 4.
- o 5.

List five beautiful words that you need to hear more often so you can heal your heart's wounds.

- o 1.
- o 2.
- o 3.
- o 4.
- o 5.

List five words that you need to forget so you can heal your heart's wounds.

- o 1.
- o 2.
- o 3.
- o 4.
- o 5.

What do you want to prune away from your heart? Journal your thoughts.

_____

_____

_____

_____

_____

_____

_____

_____

Write down two things that make you feel at ease while you are on your healing journey.

_____

_____

_____

_____

_____

_____

_____

_____

_____

_____

*Prune away everything
that stops you
from blooming.*

**Complete the following sentences as you want.
When I heal my heart, I reclaim my power,
which is...**

_____

_____

_____

**I am on the right path of my healing journey
when I feel...**

_____

_____

_____

**What would make your healing process
smoother? Journal your thoughts.**

_____

_____

_____

_____

_____

_____

_____

_____

What slows down your healing process?

_____

_____

_____

_____

_____

_____

_____

How do you show love and compassion to yourself during your healing process?

_____

_____

_____

_____

_____

_____

_____

_____

_____

How much time are you willing to spend on your healing process? Why?

_____

_____

_____

_____

_____

_____

_____

Do you think that time is your friend in your healing process? Journal your thoughts.

_____

_____

_____

_____

_____

_____

_____

_____

_____

List the most important allies in your healing process. Journal your thoughts.

_____

_____

_____

_____

_____

_____

_____

Do you have patience with yourself during your healing process? Journal your thoughts.

_____

_____

_____

_____

_____

_____

_____

_____

_____

Write about your best self-awareness habit that helps you in your healing process.

_____

_____

_____

_____

_____

_____

_____

_____

_____

Do you think that healing your heart's wounds will make a difference in your lifestyle? Journal your thoughts.

_____

_____

_____

_____

_____

_____

_____

_____

_____

Check your favorite affirmations.

- o **Healing my heart's wounds is not an overnight process.**
- o **Healing my heart's wounds takes time.**
- o **Healing my heart's wounds builds self-awareness.**
- o **Healing my heart's wounds is a process of growth.**

Now journal your thoughts.

Journal your thoughts about the most important progress you have made since you started to heal your heart's wounds.

If you could plant anything in your heart, what would you choose?

o **A word (name it)**

_____

_____

o **A virtue (name it)**

_____

_____

o **The name of my loved one (write it down)**

_____

_____

What would you never plant in your heart? Journal your thoughts.

_____

_____

_____

_____

_____

_____

_____

_____

_____

Imagine you could plant a healing word in your heart. What word would you choose? Why?

Plant hope
in your heart's wounds.

**Imagine a healing word growing in your heart.
You water this word with positivity and passion.
Journal your thoughts.**

Imagine a healing word blooming in your heart like a pretty flower. Draw this flower as vividly as you want. It will be the flower of your heart.

Imagine you can dig into your heart. What gem would you like to find? Why? Draw this gem.

Imagine a fence of positive words that can protect the flower of your heart. Write down as many positive words as you need to build this special fence.

_____

_____

_____

_____

_____

_____

_____

_____

How do you feel about creating boundaries while you heal? Journal your thoughts.

_____

_____

_____

_____

_____

_____

_____

_____

_____

List the things or persons that force you to impose boundaries.

_____

_____

_____

_____

_____

_____

_____

If there were a magic pill for fast healing, how would you like to name it?

_____

_____

_____

What has been your soul medicine during your healing process?

_____

_____

_____

_____

_____

_____

If there were a poetry prescription for a broken heart like yours, what would you like to read? Journal your thoughts.

What feelings would you like to plant in your heart? Why? Journal your thoughts.

When you heal your hidden wounds,
you learn to garden your heart.

What feelings would you like to see blooming in your heart? Why? Journal your thoughts.

_____

_____

_____

_____

_____

_____

_____

_____

_____

Journal your thoughts about the actual progress you made while healing your heart's wounds.

_____

_____

_____

_____

_____

_____

_____

_____

Imagine your heart is fully healed. Draw an extraordinary self-portrait. Be as crazy, angry, or sweet as you want.

Check your favorite affirmation.
- ○ **Healing my heart's wounds makes me feel grateful.**
- ○ **Healing my heart's wounds helps me accept myself.**
- ○ **Healing my heart's wounds helps me love myself more.**

Now journal your thoughts.

Can you beautifully visualize yourself in the next years? Describe your future self with positive words. Draw a lovely self-portrait.

What emotional advice would you give to your future self? Journal your thoughts.

_____

_____

_____

_____

_____

_____

_____

_____

Write about your favorite practice that helps you connect with your inner needs.

_____

_____

_____

_____

_____

_____

_____

_____

_____

_____

Ask yourself, "Where to from here?" Write down your dreams for the coming years.

_____

_____

_____

_____

_____

_____

_____

_____

What do you want to do most with your life after healing your wounds?

_____

_____

_____

_____

_____

_____

_____

_____

_____

What is the most beautiful thing that you found within yourself during your healing process? Journal your thoughts.

_____

_____

_____

_____

_____

_____

_____

_____

Do you feel more connected with your heart after healing your hidden wounds? Why?

_____

_____

_____

_____

_____

_____

_____

_____

Be kind
and you will always look beautiful.

What is the biggest lesson that you learned from your healing process?

Do you think that healing is part of your identity from now on? Why? Be honest.

Complete the following sentences as you want.
Dear Heart, tell me how...

_____

_____

_____

_____

Dear Heart, let me know what...

_____

_____

_____

_____

Dear Heart, talk with me about...

_____

_____

_____

_____

Dear Heart, I am right here if...

_____

_____

_____

_____

_____

What impact do you think you will have on other people's lives after healing your inner wounds?

_____

_____

_____

_____

_____

_____

_____

_____

List the most important things that you want to do for others as a person who has already gone through a healing process.

_____

_____

_____

_____

_____

_____

_____

_____

What would you like to do for others to help them focus on healing and self-exploration?

_____

_____

_____

_____

_____

_____

_____

_____

What will you say to others to encourage them in their healing process? Be honest.

_____

_____

_____

_____

_____

_____

_____

_____

_____

What will you allow yourself to do emotionally from now on?

_____

_____

_____

_____

_____

_____

_____

_____

Will you make a daily habit of working on yourself to heal and grow more?

_____

_____

_____

_____

_____

_____

_____

_____

_____

What choices will you make so you can preserve your healing achievements?

*I truly believe
that healing is all about love.*

DEAR READER,

Thank you very much for completing this journal for healing.

I hope that my questions, poems, and affirmations helped you heal your hidden wounds, focus on the beauty of your heart, nurture your most important values, and find a healthy way to improve your life. If so, please take a moment and show your appreciation by writing a short Amazon review on the website where you purchased this journal. Your kindness means the world to me. Thank you very much, beautiful soul.

May my poems and healing affirmations grow roots in your heart. I hope that one day, they will make you bloom with love.

With hope, love, and poetry,
Alexandra

ABOUT THE AUTHOR

Alexandra Vasiliu is an award-winning poet and a believer in the healing power of love.

She has been composing poems for as long as she can remember.

She has a Ph.D. in Medieval Literature and is the author of the uplifting poetry collections *Blooming, Be My Moon,* and *Healing Words*.

When she isn't busy writing poetry books, she loves reading healing poems, admiring the beautiful sunset at the beach, collecting seashells, and drinking fruit tea from a colorful mug.

Stay connected to her on Instagram @alexandravasiliuwriter.

Learn more about Alexandra at alexandravasiliu.net.